THE ULTIMATE GREEK PHRASEBOOK

Everything that you will need during your stay in Greece.

by Alexander F. Rondos

Alexander F. Rondos

This publication is designed to provide accurate and authoritative information with regard to the subject matter covered. It is sold with the understanding that the publisher is not engaged in rendering legal, accounting, or other professional advice. If legal advice or other expert assistance is required, the services of a competent professional person should be sought.

Copyright © 2016 XpressEpublishing, Alexader F. Rondos
All rights reserved.
ISBN-13: 978-1500995355
ISBN-10: 1500995355
This book, or parts thereof, may not be reproduced in any form without permission from the author.
xpressepublishing@gmail.com

TABLE OF CONTENTS

INTRODUCTION	*4*
INSTRUCTIONS	*6*
BASIC COMMUNICATION AND GREETINGS	*8*
Relatives	*16*
NUMBERS	*19*
DAYS OF THE WEEK / TIME	*22*
TRAVELING/DIRECTIONS/ ACCOMODATION	*25*
FOOD/DRINK	*37*
SHOPPING	*46*
BUSINESS	*50*
EMERGENCY	*56*
DESCRIPTIONS	*60*
Weather	*66*
GESTURES	*68*
Negative meaning	*68*
Neutral	*70*
No meaning	*70*
IMPORTANT THINGS TO KNOW	*73*
FREE E-BOOK "EXPLORE SECRET GREECE" PROMOTION	*78*

INTRODUCTION

This handbook is the best companion for people travelling to Greece for tourism or business, or just want to learn the basics for communication in Greek, and also important things to know about Greece and Greek people. Written by local Greek experts, it contains carefully selected words and phrases, which will make your everyday communication with the locals much easier, and your stay in Greece much more pleasant. Impress the locals and make them friendlier towards you, understand all the basics in signs, menus and oral expressions, avoid misunderstandings, and of course learn how to communicate in case of an emergency. From basic communication and greetings to expressions for directions, food, shopping, emergency, business and much more, it will be your valuable digital companion, accompanying you every day of your stay.

All the words and phrases are first given in English, then phonetically in Greek in order for you to know how to pronounce them, and then in transliteration, so you can understand them if you see them written.

It even contains a chapter dedicated in selected gestures and how the locals perceive them, in order to avoid misunderstandings. A final chapter of important things to know and useful contact numbers completes the basic knowledge anyone must have before travelling to Greece.

Please feel free to contact us for any comment, enquiry or add-ons you might want to see in a book like this.

INSTRUCTIONS

With this book, you will be able to pronounce Greek like a local Greek. You will not find this kind of method anywhere else, not in a book or in the internet. The phonetic writing system used in this book was invented by our team, it is very easy to follow, and results in true Greek pronunciation.

Here are some instructions on how to use this book, and explanation of the simple rules we followed, to make it as easy as possible for you to understand and pronounce Greek correctly.

First you will see the English word or phrase, then phonetically in Greek in order for you to know how to pronounce it, and then in transliteration, so you can understand it if you see it written. The English word is always bold.

Greek words have overtones in vowels, in order for the speaker to know where to tone each word. In order to make it easy and practical for you, we made these vowels bold and underlined. So, in each word with more than one vowel, you will see a vowel that is bold and underlined. That means you must tone this word in that letter. So for example in the word "parakal**o**", which means "please", you tone the word on the "o." Some words need to be toned in two different vowels within the same word.

Also, when you see bold "**th**" in a word it means you must pronounce it like you do in word "the", while when you see it without bold, like "th", you must pronounce it like you do in the word "through".

Moreover, when you see "**wh**" you must pronounce it like in the word "**wh**at". Also, pronounce all "i" like the word "**i**n**i**t**i**ally" and not like the word "**i**ce", and all "e" like in the word "**e**stimation" and not like in the word "bee".

A few selected words and phrases are intentionally repeated in different chapters of this book, because they can be useful to you in more than one occasion, which are applicable in different chapters of this book.

Lastly, remember that the Greeks do not pronounce the letter "r" like the English or the Americans, but more like the Scottish.

BASIC COMMUNICATION AND GREETINGS

Hello	Γεια σας
	[y<u>a</u>sas]
Do you speak English?	Μιλάτε Αγγλικά;
	[mil<u>a</u>te aglik<u>a</u>?]
I don't understand	Δεν καταλαβαίνω
	[**th**en katalav<u>e</u>no]
I don't speak Greek	Δεν μιλάω ελληνικά
	[**th**en mil<u>a</u>o elinik<u>a</u>]
I don't understand Greek	Δεν καταλαβαίνω ελληνικά
	[**th**en katalav<u>e</u>no elinik<u>a</u>]
Can you speak more slowly?	Μπορείτε να μιλήσετε πιο αργά;
	[bor<u>i</u>te na mil<u>i</u>sete pio ar**wh**<u>a</u>?]
Could you repeat (that), please?	Μπορείτε να επαναλάβετε παρακαλώ;
	[bor<u>i</u>te na epanal<u>a</u>vete, parakal<u>o</u>?]

The Ultimate Greek Phrasebook

Yes	Ναι
	[ne]
No	Όχι
	[ohi]
Ok	Εντάξει
	[entaksi]
Please	Παρακαλώ
	[parakalo]
Excuse me	Με συγχωρείτε
	[me synhorite]
Sorry	Συγνώμη
	[siwhnomi]
Pardon me	Με συγχωρείτε
	[me synhorite]
Ok/fine no problem	Εντάξει κανένα πρόβλημα
	[entaksi kanena provlima]
Good morning	Καλημέρα
	[kalimera]
Good evening	Καλό απόγευμα

	[kal**o** ap**o**yevma]
Goodnight	Καληνύχτα
	[kalin_i_hta]
Goodbye	Αντίο
	[ant_i_o]
Thank you	Ευχαριστώ
	[efharist**o**]
No, thank you	Όχι, ευχαριστώ
	[**o**xi, efharist**o**]
Thank you very much	Ευχαριστώ πολύ
	[efharist**o** pol_i_]
Thank you for your help	Ευχαριστώ για την βοήθειά σας
	[efharist**o** ya tin vo_i_thi_a_ sas]
You're welcome	Παρακαλώ
	[parakal**o**]
My name is ____	[to **o**nom**a** mu _i_ne____]
	Το όνομά μου είναι____
What's your name?	Πως ονομάζεσαι;

The Ultimate Greek Phrasebook

	[pos onom<u>a</u>zese?]
I am pleased to meet you	Χαίρομαι που σας γνωρίζω
	[h<u>e</u>rome pu sas **wh**nor<u>i</u>zo]
How are you?	Πως είστε?
	[pos <u>i</u>ste?]
I am fine thanks and you?	Είμαι καλά ευχαριστώ, εσείς?
	[<u>i</u>me kal<u>a</u> efharist<u>o</u>, es<u>i</u>s?]
Fine	Εντάξει
	[ent<u>a</u>ksi]
Very well	Καλά
	[kal<u>a</u>]
Where do you live?	Που μένετε?
	[pu m<u>e</u>nete]
I live in____	Μένω στην____
	[m<u>e</u>no stin____]
See you soon	Τα λέμε σύντομα
	[ta l<u>e</u>me s<u>i</u>ntoma]
This is my friend	Αυτός είναι ο φίλος μου

	[aft**o**s **i**ne o f**i**los mu]
This is my boyfriend	Αυτός είναι ο σύντροφός μου
	[aft**o**s **i**ne o s**i**ntrof**o**s mu]
This is my girlfriend	Αυτή είναι η σύντροφός μου
	[aft**i** **i**ne i s**i**ntrof**o**s mu]
This is my husband	Αυτός είναι ο σύζυγός μου
	[aft**o**s **i**ne o s**i**ziwh**o**s mu]
This is my wife	Αυτή είναι η σύζυγός μου
	[aft**i** **i**ne i s**i**ziwh**o**s mu]
Man	Άνδρας
	[anth**r**as]
Woman	Γυναίκα
	[yin**e**ka]
Come visit me	Ελάτε να με επισκεφθείτε
	[el**a**te na me episkefth**i**te]
I had a wonderful time	Πέρασα υπέροχα
	[p**e**rasa ip**e**roha]

The Ultimate Greek Phrasebook

Where is the subway?	Που είναι το μετρό;
	[pu ine to metro]
How much does that cost?	Πόσο κοστίζει αυτό;
	[poso kostizi afto?]
Do you have _____	Έχετε _____
	[ehete _____]
Is there a phone I can use?	Υπάρχει τηλέφωνο που να μπορώ να χρησιμοποιήσω;
	[iparhi tilefono pu na boro na hrisimopiiso?]
Can I get online?	Μπορώ να μπω στο ιντερνετ;
	[boro na bo sto internet?]
Can you help me, please?	Μπορείτε να με βοηθήσετε παρακαλώ;
	[borite na me voithisete parakalo?]
Where is the toilet please?	Που είναι η τουαλέτα παρακαλώ;
	[pu ine i tualeta parakalo?]
Can someone assist	Μπορεί κάποιος να μας

us?	βοηθήσει?
	[bor**i** k**a**pios na mas voith**i**si?]
Do you need help?	Χρειάζεστε βοήθεια?
	[hri**a**zeste vo**i**thia?]
It is hot isn't it?	Έχει ζέστη, έτσι δεν είναι?
	[**e**hi z**e**sti, **e**tsi den **i**ne?]
Could you take us/me a picture please	Μπορείτε να μας/με βγάλετε μία φωτογραφία παρακαλώ
	[bor**i**te na mas/me vwh**a**lete m**i**a fotowhraf**i**a parakal**o**]
Maybe	Ίσως
	[**i**sos]
Right	Σωστά
	[sost**a**]
Wrong	Λάθος
	[l**a**thos]
Here	Εδώ
	[eth**o**]
There	Εκεί
	[ek**i**]

I would like	Θα ήθελα
	[tha ithela]
I want	Θέλω
	[thelo]
I do not want	Δεν θέλω
	[then thelo]
Danger	Κίνδυνος
	[kinthinos]
Who	Ποιος
	[pios]
What	Τι
	[ti]
When	Πότε
	[pote]
Where	Που
	[pu]
Why	Γιατί
	[yati]
How	Πως

	[pos]
What happened?	Τι συνέβη;
	[ti sin<u>e</u>vi?]
I am	Είμαι
	[<u>i</u>me]
You are	Είσαι
	[<u>i</u>se]
He/she is	Αυτός/Αυτή είναι
	[aft<u>o</u>s/aft<u>i</u> <u>i</u>ne]
We are	Εμείς είμαστε
	[em<u>i</u>s <u>i</u>maste]
They are	Αυτοί είναι
	[aft<u>i</u> <u>i</u>ne]

Relatives

Father	Πατέρας
	[pat<u>e</u>ras]
Mother	Μητέρα
	[mit<u>e</u>ra]
Dad	Μπαμπάς
	[bab<u>a</u>s]

The Ultimate Greek Phrasebook

Mom	Μαμά
	[mam**a**]
Aunt	Θεία
	[th**i**a]
Uncle	Θείος
	[th**i**os]
Brother	Αδελφός
	[athelf**o**s]
Sister	Αδελφή
	[athelf**i**]
Child	Παιδί
	[peth**i**]
Children	Παιδιά
	[peth**ia**]
Cousin	Ξάδελφος
	[ks**a**thelfos]
Daughter	Κόρη
	[k**o**ri]
Son	Γιος
	[yos]
Family	Οικογένεια
	[ikoy**e**nia]
Grandfather	Παππούς
	[pap**us**]
Grandmother	Γιαγιά

	[yay**a**]
Husband	Ο Σύζυγος
	[o s**i**ziwhos]
Man	Άνδρας
	[**a**nthras]
Men	Άνδρες
	[**a**nthres]
Wife	Η Σύζυγος
	[i s**i**ziwhos]
Woman	Γυναίκα
	[yin**e**ka]
Women	Γυναίκες
	[yin**e**kes]

NUMBERS

0 zero	**Μηδέν**
	[mith<u>e</u>n]
1 one	Ένα
	[<u>e</u>na]
2 two	Δύο
	[th<u>i</u>o]
3 three	Τρία
	[tr<u>i</u>a]
4 four	Τέσσερα
	[t<u>e</u>sera]
5 five	Πέντε
	[p<u>e</u>nde]
6 six	Έξι
	[<u>e</u>ksi]
7 seven	Επτά
	[ept<u>a</u>]
8 eight	Οκτώ
	[okt<u>o</u>]
9 nine	Εννιά
	[eni<u>a</u>]
10 ten	Δέκα
	[th<u>e</u>ka]
11 eleven	Έντεκα

	[entheka]
12 twelve	Δώδεκα
	[thotheka]
13 thirteen	Δεκατρία
	[thekatria]
14 fourteen	Δεκατέσσερα
	[thekatesera]
15 fifteen	Δεκαπέντε
	[thekapende]
16 sixteen	Δεκαέξι
	[thekaeksi]
17 seventeen	Δεκαεπτά
	[thekaepta]
18 eighteen	Δεκαοχτώ
	[thekaokto]
19 nineteen	Δεκαεννιά
	[thekaenia]
20 twenty	Είκοσι
	[ikosi]
100 a hundred	Εκατό
	[ekato]
1000 a thousand	Χίλια
	[hilia]
10000 ten thousand	Δέκα χιλιάδες
	[theka hiliathes]

100.000 one hundred thousand	Εκατό χιλιάδες
	[ekato hiliathes]
1.000.000 one million	Ένα εκατομμύριο
	[ena ekatomirio]
Plus	Συν
	[sin]
Minus	Μείον
	[mion]
More (than)	Περισσότερο (από)
	[perisotero (apo)]
Less (than)	Λιγότερο (από)
	[liwhotero (apo)]
Approximately	Περίπου
	[peripu]
First	Πρώτος
	[protos]
Second	Δεύτερος
	[thefteros]
Third	Τρίτος
	[tritos]

DAYS OF THE WEEK / TIME

Monday	Δευτέρα
	[theft**e**ra]
Tuesday	Τρίτη
	[tr**i**ti]
Wednesday	Τετάρτη
	[tet**a**rti]
Thursday	Πέμπτη
	[p**e**mti]
Friday	Παρασκευή
	[paraskev**i**]
Saturday	Σάββατο
	[s**a**vato]
Sunday	Κυριακή
	[kiriak**i**]
Yesterday	Εχθές
	[exth**e**s]
Today	Σήμερα
	[s**i**mera]
Tomorrow	Αύριο
	[**a**vrio]
Day	Ημέρα
	[im**e**ra]
Night	Νύχτα

The Ultimate Greek Phrasebook

	[nihta]
Week	Εβδομάδα
	[evthomatha]
Month	Μήνας
	[minas]
Year	Έτος/Χρόνος
	[etos/hronos]
Second	Δευτερόλεπτο
	[thefterolepto]
Minute	Λεπτό
	[lepto]
Hour	Ώρα
	[ora]
Morning	Πρωί
	[proi]
Evening	Βράδυ
	[vrathi]
Noon	Μεσημέρι
	[mesimeri]
Afternoon	Απόγευμα
	[apoyevma]
Midnight	Μεσάνυχτα
	[mesanihta]
Now	Τώρα
	[tora]

Later	Αργότερα
	[ar**who**tera]

TRAVELING/DIRECTIONS/ ACCOMODATION

Where can I find a bus/taxi?	Που μπορώ να βρω ένα λεωφορείο/ταξί;
	[pu boro na vro ena leoforio/taksi]
Does this bus go to____?	Πηγαίνει αυτό το λεωφορείο στο____;
	[piyeni afto to leoforio sto____?]
Where can I find a train/metro?	Που είναι το τρένο/μετρό;
	[pu ine to treno/metro?]
Can I have a map of the city, please?	Μπορώ να έχω έναν χάρτη της πόλης, παρακαλώ;
	[boro na eho enan harti tis polis, parakalo?]
Can I have a subway map, please?	Μπορώ να έχω έναν χάρτη του μετρό, παρακαλώ;
	[boro na eho enan harti tu metro, parakalo]
Can you take me to the airport please?	Μπορείτε να με πάτε στο αεροδρόμιο, παρακαλώ;
	[borite na me pate sto aerothromio, parakalo?]
Take me to this address, please	Πηγαίνετέ με σε αυτήν την διεύθυνση παρακαλώ

	[piy**e**net**e** me se aftin tin thi**e**fthinsi, parakal**o**]
What is the fare?	Πόσο κοστίζει το εισητήριο;
	[p**o**so kost**i**zi to isit**i**rio?]
Stop here, please	Σταματήστε εδώ, παρακαλώ
	[stamat**i**ste eth**o** parakal**o**]
Can you show me on the map how to get there?	Μπορείτε να μου δείξετε στον χάρτη πως να πάω εκεί;
	[bor**i**te na mu **th**iksete ston h**a**rti pos na p**a**o ek**i**?]
Will you please write that down for me?	Θα το γράψετε αυτό παρακαλώ;
	[tha to **whr**apsete aft**o** parakal**o**?]
Where is the exit?	Που είναι η έξοδος;
	[pu **i**ne i **e**ksothos?]
Where is the bathroom please?	Που είναι το μπάνιο παρακαλω;
	[pu **i**ne to b**a**nio, parakal**o**?]
Is it nearby?	Είναι κοντά;
	[**i**ne kond**a**?]
Is it far?	Είναι μακριά;
	[**i**ne makri**a**?]
Go straight ahead	Πηγαίνετε ευθεία

	[piyenete efthia]
Go that way	Πηγαίνετε από εκεί
	[piyenete apo eki]
Go back	Πηγαίνετε πίσω
	[piyenete piso]
Turn right	Στρίψτε δεξιά
	[stripste deksia]
Turn left	Στρίψτε αριστερά
	[stripste aristera]
You turn	Θα στρίψετε
	[tha stripsete]
You go	Θα πάτε
	[tha pate]
It's	Είναι
	[ine]
(On the) right	(στα) δεξιά
	[(sta) deksia]
(On the) left	(στα) αριστερά
	[(sta) aristera]
Straight on	Ευθεία
	[efthia]
Near	Κοντά
	[konda]
Where's the best beach?	Που βρίσκεται η καλύτερη παραλία;

	[pu vriskete I kaliteri paralia?]
How do I get to the swimming pool?	Πως πάω στην πισίνα?
	[pos pao stin pisina?]
Left	Αριστερά
	[aristera]
Right	Δεξιά
	[theksia]
Straight ahead	Ευθεία
	[efthia]
I'm lost	Έχω χαθεί
	[eho hathi]
Hotel	Ξενοδοχείο
	[ksenothohio]
We must spend the night here	Θα πρέπει να περάσουμε τη νύχτα εδώ
	[tha prepi na perasume ti nihta etho]
I want to book a room	Θέλω να κλείσω ένα δωμάτιο
	[thelo na kliso ena thomatio]
One night/four nights	Μία νύχτα/ τέσσερις νύχτες
	[mia nihta/teseris nihtes]
Until	Μέχρι
	[mehri]

A double room	Ένα δίκλινο
	[ena thiklino]
A single room	Ένα μονόκλινο
	[ena monoklino]
With bathroom	Με μπάνιο
	[me banio]
With shower	Με ντους
	[me ntus]
With a view	Με θέα
	[me thea]
Can I have____?	Μπορώ να έχω____
	[boro na eho____?]
Your passports	Τα διαβατήριά σας
	[ta thiavatiria sas]
Excuse me	Με συγχωρείτε
	[me sinhorite]
Sorry	Συγγνώμη
	[siwhnomi]
Where is	Που είναι
	[pu ine]
I'd like to hire a boat	Θα ήθελα να νοικιάσω μία βάρκα
	[tha ithela na nikiaso mia varka]
Do you have suncream?	Έχετε αντηλιακό?

	[ehete antiliako]
I'd like to hire a pedalo	Θα ήθελα να νοικιάσω ένα ποδήλατο θαλάσσης
	[tha ithela na nikiaso ena pothilato thalasis]
Is it safe for children to swim here?	Είναι ασφαλές για παιδιά να κολυμπούν εδώ;
	[ine asfales ya pethia na kolibun etho?]
One ice cream and one lolly please	Ένα παγωτό και ένα ξυλάκι γρανίτα
	[ena pawhoto qe ena ksilaki whranita]
Where can we dive?	Που μπορούμε να κάνουμε κατάδυση;
	[pu borume na kanume katathisi?]
Where can we surf?	Που μπορούμε να κάνουμε σερφ;
	[pu borume na kanume surf]
Have you got parasols	Έχετε ομπρέλες για την θάλασσα;
	[ehete obreles ya tin thalasa?]
Do you have a table outside please?	Έχετε ένα τραπέζι να καθίσουμε έξω;
	[ehete ena trapezi na kathisoume ekso?]
No ice please	Χωρίς πάγο παρακαλώ
	[horis pawho parakalo]

Where?	Που
	[pu]
Excuse me, where is____?	Με συγχωρείτε, που είναι__
	[me sinhorite, pu ine____?]
Is there a dining facility here?	Υπάρχει κάποιο εστιατόριο εδώ κοντά?
	[iparxi kapio estiatorio etho konda?]
How many kilometers to the nearest town?	Πόσα χιλιόμετρα μέχρι την κοντινότερη πόλη?
	[posa hiliometra mehri tin kondinoteri poli?]
Are there any hotels near here?	Υπάρχουν καθόλου ξενοδοχεία εδώ κοντά?
	[iparhun katholu ksenothohia etho konda?]
Are there any restaurants near here?	Υπάρχουν καθόλου εστιατόρια εδώ κοντά?
	[iparhun katholu estiatoria etho konda?]
We want to go to____	Θέλουμε να πάμε στο____
	[thelume na pame sto____]
Are there rental cars available?	Υπάρχουν αυτοκίνητα προς ενοικίαση διαθέσιμα?

	[ip**a**rhun aftok**i**nita pros enik**i**asi thiath**e**sima?]
Is there a telephone available?	Υπάρχει διαθέσιμο τηλέφωνο;
	[ip**a**rxi thiath**e**simo til**e**fono?]
Beach	Παραλία
	[paral**i**a]
Border	Σύνορα
	[s**i**nora]
Bridge	Γέφυρα
	[y**e**fira]
Camp	Κατασκήνωση
	[katask**i**nosi]
Dirt road	Χωματόδρομος
	[homat**o**thromos]
Forest	Δάσος
	[th**a**sos]
Harbor	Λιμάνι
	[lim**a**ni]
Hill	Λόφος
	[l**o**fos]
House	Σπίτι
	[sp**i**ti]
Lake	Λίμνη
	[l**i**mni]

The Ultimate Greek Phrasebook

Mountain	Βουνό
	[vun**o**]
Ocean	Ωκεανός
	[okean**o**s]
Path	Μονοπάτι
	[monop**a**ti]
Paved road	Ασφαλτοστρωμένος δρόμος
	[asfaltostrom**e**nos thr**o**mos]
Place	Μέρος
	[m**e**ros]
Position	Σημείο
	[sim**i**o]
Sea	Θάλασσα
	[th**a**lasa]
Square	Πλατεία
	[plat**i**a]
Tree	Δέντρο
	[th**e**ndro]
Valley	Κοιλάδα
	[kil**a**tha]
Village	Χωριό
	[hori**o**]
Where	Που
	[pu]

Above/over	Επάνω
	[ep<u>a</u>no]
After/past	Μετά
	[met<u>a</u>]
Back/behind	Πίσω
	[p<u>i</u>so]
Before/in front of/forward	Μπροστά
	[brost<u>a</u>]
Between	Ενδιάμεσα
	[enthi<u>a</u>mesa]
Coordinates	Συντεταγμένες
	[sintetagm<u>e</u>nes]
Degrees	Μοίρες
	[m<u>i</u>res]
Down	Κάτω
	[k<u>a</u>to]
Far	Μακριά
	[makri<u>a</u>]
Longitude	Γεωγραφικό μήκος
	[yeografik<u>o</u> m<u>i</u>kos]
Latitude	Γεωγραφικό πλάτος
	[yeografik<u>o</u> pl<u>a</u>tos]
My position is____	Η θέση μου είναι____
	[I th<u>e</u>si mu <u>i</u>ne___]

Near	Κοντά
	[kond**a**]
North	Βόρεια
	[v**o**ria]
Northeast	Βορειοανατολικά
	[vorioanatolik**a**]
Northwest	Βορειοδυτικά
	[vorio**thi**tik**a**]
West	Δυτικά
	[**thi**tik**a**]
East	Ανατολικά
	[anatolik**a**]
South	Νότια
	[n**o**tia]
Southeast	Νοτιοανατολικά
	[notioanatolik**a**]
Southwest	Νοτιοδυτικά
	[notio**thi**tik**a**]
Straight ahead	Ευθεία
	[efth**i**a]
Under	Κάτω
	[k**a**to]
Up	Επάνω
	[ep**a**no]
Gasoline	Βενζίνη

	[venzini]
Diesel	Πετρέλαιο
	[petreleo]
Gas	Αέριο
	[aerio]
Liters	Λίτρα
	[litra]
Do you have____	Έχετε____
	[ehete____]
We need____	Χρειαζόμαστε____
	[hriazomaste]

FOOD/DRINK

Where is the bathroom please?	Που είναι το μπάνιο παρακαλώ?
	[pu ine to banio parakalo]
Where can I get something to eat?	Που μπορώ να πάρω κάτι να φάω
	[pu boro na paro kati na fao?]
Is there a good restaurant around here?	Υπάρχει κάποιο καλό εστιατόριο εδώ κοντά?
	[iparhi kapio kalo estiatorio etho konda?]
What will you have?	Τι θα πάρετε?
	[ti tha parete?]
I want	Θέλω
	[thelo]
I would like something to drink	Θα ήθελα κάτι να πιω
	[tha ithela kati na pio]
A glass of water, please	Ένα ποτήρι νερό παρακαλώ
	[ena potiri nero, parakalo]
A cup of tea, please	Ένα φλυτζάνι τσάι παρακαλώ
	[ena flitzani tsai, parakalo]
Coffee with milk	Καφέ με γάλα

	[kaf**e** me g**a**la]
A bottle of water	Ένα μπουκάλι νερό
	[**e**na buk**a**li ner**o**]
A beer	Μία μπύρα
	[m**i**a b**i**ra]
A greek coffee	Έναν ελληνικό καφέ
	[**e**nan elinik**o** kaf**e**]
A bottle of wine	Ένα μπουκάλι κρασί
	[**e**na buk**a**li kras**i**]
White wine	Λευκό κρασί
	[lefk**o** kras**i**]
Red wine	Κόκκινο κρασί
	[k**o**kino kras**i**]
I like it	Μου αρέσει
	[mu ar**e**si]
I don't like it	Δεν μου αρέσει
	[**th**en mu ar**e**si]
The bill please	Τον λογαριασμό παρακαλώ
	[ton lowhariasm**o** parakal**o**]
Is the tip included?	Συμπεριλαμβάνεται το φιλοδώρημα?
	[siberilamv**a**nete to filoth**o**rima?]
Is there any extra charge?	Υπάρχει κάποια επιπλέον χρέωση?

	[iparhi kapia epipleon hreosi?]
A table for two, please	Ένα τραπέζι για δύο παρακαλώ
	[ena trapezi ya thio parakalo]
The menu, please	Το μενού παρακαλώ
	[to menu parakalo]
The wine list, please	Την λίστα κρασιών, παρακαλώ
	[tin lista krasion, parakalo]
Is the water drinkable?	Είναι το νερό πόσιμο;
	[ine to nero posimo?]
Wash your hands	Πλύνε τα χέρια σου
	[pline ta heria su]
Is the food fresh?	Είναι το φαγητό φρέσκο;
	[ine to fayito fresko?]
Do you have vegetarian dishes?	Έχετε πιάτα για χορτοφάγους;
	[ehete piata ya hortofawhus?]
Appetizers	Ορεκτικά
	[orektika]
Main course	Κυρίως πιάτο
	[kirios piato]
Dessert	Επιδόρπιο
	[epithorpio]

That's all	Αυτά
	[aft**a**]
Breakfast	Πρωινό
	[proin**o**]
Lunch	Μεσημεριανό
	[mesimerian**o**]
Dinner	Δείπνο/Βραδυνό
	[th**i**pno/vrathin**o**]
Enjoy the meal!	Απολαύστε το γεύμα σας!
	[apol**a**fste to y**e**vma sas!]
Cheers!	Στην υγειά μας!
	[stin iy**a** mas!]
It's delicious!	Είναι πεντανόστιμο!
	[**i**ne pendan**o**stimo!]
Ice cubes	Παγάκια
	[pawh**a**kia]
Salt	Αλάτι
	[al**a**ti]
Pepper	Πιπέρι
	[pip**e**ri]
Sugar	Ζάχαρη
	[z**a**hari]
Soup	Σούπα
	[s**u**pa]
Salad	Σαλάτα

	[salata]
Bread	Ψωμί
	[psomi]
Butter	Βούτυρο
	[vutiro]
Rice	Ρύζι
	[rizi]
Cheese	Τυρί
	[tiri]
Vegetables	Λαχανικά
	[lahanika]
Chicken	Κοτόπουλο
	[kotopulo]
Grilled chicken	Κοτόπουλο σχάρας
	[kotopulo sharas]
Pork	Χοιρινό
	[hirino]
Beef	Μοσχάρι
	[moshari]
I like my steak rare	Θέλω την μπριζόλα μου μισοψημένη
	[thelo tin brizola mu misopsimeni]
I like my steak medium	Θέλω την μπριζόλα μου κανονική
	[thelo tin brizola mu kanonika psimeni]

I like my steak well-done	Θέλω την μπριζόλα μου καλοψημένη
	[thelo tin brizola mu kalopsimeni]
Juice	Χυμός
	[himos]
Pie	Πίτα
	[pita]
Ice cream	Παγωτό
	[pawhoto]
Another, please	Ακόμη ένα παρακαλώ
	[akomi ena, parakalo]
More, please	Κι άλλο παρακαλώ
	[qialo parakalo]
Pass the____please	Δώσε μου το___παρακαλώ
	[dose mu to____parakalo]
Spicy	Πικάντικο
	[pikandiko]
Sweet	Γλυκό
	[whliko]
Sour	Ξινό
	[ksino]
Food	Φαγητό
	[fayito]
Can	Κονσέρβα
	[konserva]

The Ultimate Greek Phrasebook

Cup	Κούπα
	[k<u>u</u>pa]
Plate	Πιάτο
	[pi<u>a</u>to]
Fork	Πηρούνι
	[pir<u>u</u>ni]
Knife	Μαχαίρι
	[mah<u>e</u>ri]
Spoon	Κουτάλι
	[kut<u>a</u>li]
Napkin	Χαρτοπετσέτα
	[hartopets<u>e</u>ta]
Glass	Ποτήρι
	[pot<u>i</u>ri]
Beans	Φασόλια
	[fas<u>o</u>lia]
Bread	Ψωμί
	[psom<u>i</u>]
Butter	Βούτυρο
	[v<u>u</u>tiro]
Cheese	Τυρί
	[tir<u>i</u>]
Coffee	Καφές
	[kaf<u>e</u>s]
Fish	Ψάρι

	[ps<u>a</u>ri]
Flour	Αλεύρι
	[al<u>e</u>vri]
Fruit	Φρούτο
	[fr<u>u</u>to]
Meat	Κρέας
	[kr<u>e</u>as]
Milk	Γάλα
	[wh<u>a</u>la]
Oil	Λάδι
	[l<u>a</u>thi]
Potatoes	Πατάτες
	[pat<u>a</u>tes]
Salt	Αλάτι
	[al<u>a</u>ti]
Soup	Σούπα
	[s<u>u</u>pa]
Sugar	Ζάχαρη
	[z<u>a</u>hari]
Tea	Τσάι
	[ts<u>ai</u>]
Water	Νερό
	[ner<u>o</u>]
Wine	Κρασί
	[kr<u>asi</u>]

The Ultimate Greek Phrasebook

Drink (noun)	Ποτό
	[pot_o_]
Eat	Τρώω
	[tr_o_o]
Tomato	Τομάτα
	[tom_a_ta]
Aubergine	[melitz_a_na]

SHOPPING

Let's go shopping!	**Πάμε για ψώνια!**
	[pame ya psonia!]
Euro/Euros	Ευρώ
	[evro/evro]
Rate of exchange	Ισοτιμία
	[isotimia]
Exchange office	Ανταλλακτήριο
	[andalaktirio]
Receipt	Απόδειξη
	[apothiksi]
How much does this cost?	Πόσο κοστίζει αυτό?
	[poso kostizi afto?]
It's too expensive	Είναι πολύ ακριβό
	[ine poli akrivo]
Can you give better price?	Μπορείτε να κάνετε καλύτερη τιμή?
	[borite na kanete kaliteri timi?]
Do you take credit cards?	Δέχεστε πιστωτικές κάρτες?
	[theheste pistotikes kartes?]
I'd like to pay in cash	Θα ήθελα να πληρώσω με μετρητά

	[tha ithela na pliroso me metrita]
I'd like to pay by credit card	Θα ήθελα να πληρώσω με πιστωτική κάρτα
	[tha ithela na pliroso me pistotiki karta]
Can I order this online?	Μπορώ να το παραγγείλω από το ίντερνετ?
	[boro na to paragilo afto apo to internet?]
Would you have_____	Μήπως έχετε____
	[mipos exete____]
One kilo	Ένα κιλό
	[ena kilo]
Two kilos	Δύο Κιλά
	[thio kila]
That's all	Αυτά
	[afta]
Together	Μαζί
	[mazi]
At what time does the store open?	Τι ώρα ανοίγει το μαγαζί?
	[ti ora aniyi to mawhazi?]
At what time does the store close?	Τι ώρα κλείνει το μαγαζί?
	[ti ora klini to mawhazi?]
What would you like?	Τι θα θέλατε?

	[ti tha thelate?]
Can I help you?	Μπορώ να σας βοηθήσω;
	[boro na sas voithiso?]
I would like (to buy) this	Θα ήθελα (να αγοράσω) αυτό
	[tha ithela (na awhoraso) afto]
Here it is	Νάτο
	[nato]
Is that all?	Αυτά είναι όλα;
	[afta ine ola?]
Women's clothes	Γυναικεία ρούχα
	[yinekia ruha]
Men's clothes	Ανδρικά ρούχα
	[anthrika ruha]
Blouse	Μπλούζα
	[bluza]
Skirt	Φούστα
	[fusta]
Dress	Φόρεμα
	[forema]
Pants	Παντελόνι
	[panteloni]
Shirt	Πουκάμισο
	[pukamiso]
Tie	Γραβάτα

The Ultimate Greek Phrasebook

	[whravata]
Watch	Ρολόι
	[roloi]
Shoes and socks	Παπούτσια και κάλτσες
	[paputsia kie kaltses]
Jeans	Τζιν
	[jean]
Perfume	Άρωμα
	[aroma]
Bookstore	Βιβλιοπωλείο
	[vivliopolio]
Bakery	Φούρνος
	[furnos]
Market	Αγορά
	[awhora]
Supermarket	Σούπερμάρκετ
	[supermarket]

BUSINESS

Let's do business in Greece!	Ας κάνουμε δουλειές στην Ελλάδα!
	[as kanume thulies stin elatha!]
Where is my customs declaration?	Που είναι η τελωνειακή δήλωσή μου;
	[pu ine i teloniaki dilosi mu?]
I do not have anything to declare	Δεν έχω τίποτα να δηλώσω
	[then eho tipota na thiloso]
These goods are personal	Αυτά τα πράγματα είναι προσωπικά
	[afta ta prawhmata ine prosopika]
Not for sale	Δεν είναι προς πώληση
	[then ine pros polisi]
Can you help me fill out the forms?	Μπορείτε να με βοηθήσετε να συμπληρώσω αυτά τα έντυπα;
	[borite na me voithisete na sibliroso afta ta endipa?]
Is this correct	Είναι αυτό σωστό;
	[ine afto sosto?]
Here is my passport	Ορίστε, το διαβατήριό

	μου
	[oriste, to thiavatirio mu]
Here is my visa	Ορίστε, η βίζα μου
	[oriste, i viza mu]
I have no (target) money	Δεν έχω χρηματικό ποσό να δηλώσω
	[then eho hrimatiko poso na thiloso]
Ad valorem	Κατ' αξίαν
	[kat aksian]
Baggage	Αποσκευές
	[aposkeves]
Bill of lading	Φορτωτική
	[fortotiki]
Cargo	Φορτίο
	[fortio]
Customs	Τελωνείο
	[telonio]
Customs declaration	Τελωνειακή δήλωση
	[teloniaki thilosi]
Customs tax	Τελωνειακός φόρος
	[teloniakos foros]
Customs worker	Τελωνειακός υπάλληλος
	[teloniakos ipalilos]
Damaged	Έχει ζημιά

	[ehi zimia]
Delivery	Παράδοση
	[parathosi]
Duty	Δασμός
	[thasmos]
Expenditures	Έξοδα
	[eksotha]
Export	Εισαγωγή
	[eksawhoyi]
False	Λανθασμένος
	[lanthasmenos]
Foreign currency	Ξένο νόμισμα
	[kseno nomisma]
Form (document)	Έντυπο
	[entipo]
Holdings	Περιουσιακά στοιχεία
	[periusiaka stihia]
Import	Εισαγωγή
	[isawhoyi]
Insurance	Ασφάλεια
	[asfalia]
Loading	Φορτίο
	[fortio]
Narcotics	Ναρκωτικά
	[narkotika]

National treasure	Εθνικός θησαυρός
	[ethnik**o**s thisav**ro**s]
Nomenclature	Ονοματολογία
	[onomatoloy**ia**]
On-board	Επί του πλοίου
	[ep**i** tu pl**iu**]
Origin	Προέλευση
	[pro**e**lefsi]
Owner	Ιδιοκτήτης
	[ithiokt**i**tis]
Packing list	Κατάλογος περιεχομένων
	[kat**a**lo**wh**os periehom**e**non]
Passport	Διαβατήριο
	[thiavat**i**rio]
Permission	Άδεια
	[**a**thia]
Personal use	Προσωπική χρήση
	[prosopik**i** hr**i**si]
Personnel	Προσωπικό
	[prosopik**o**]
Prohibited	Απαγορευμένο
	[apa**wh**orevm**e**no]
Property	Περιουσία
	[perius**ia**]

Rate	Αξία
	[aks<u>i</u>a]
Receipt	Απόδειξη
	[ap<u>o</u>thiksi]
Relics	Κατάλοιπα
	[kat<u>a</u>lipa]
Restricted	Περιορισμένο
	[periorizm<u>e</u>no]
Souvenir	Ενθύμιο
	[enth<u>i</u>mio]
Specification	Προδιαγραφή
	[prothia**whraf<u>i</u>**]
Storage	Αποθήκη
	[apoth<u>i</u>ki]
Tariff	Δασμός
	[thasm<u>o</u>s]
Tax-free	Αφορολόγητο
	[aforol<u>o</u>yito]
Answer	Απαντώ
	[apant<u>o</u>]
Responsible for	Υπεύθυνος για
	[ip<u>e</u>fthinos ya]
Fill out	Συμπληρώνω
	[siblir<u>o</u>no]
Customs inspection	Τελωνειακός έλεγχος

The Ultimate Greek Phrasebook

	[teloniak**os** **e**lenhos]
Transportation	Μεταφορά
	[metafor**a**]
Unloading	Ξεφόρτωμα
	[ksef**o**rtoma]
Valuables	Τιμαλφή
	[timalf**i**]
Value	Αξία
	[aks**i**a]
Visa	Βίζα
	[v**i**za]
Weapons	Όπλα
	[**o**pla]
X-ray machine	Μηχάνημα ακτίνων Χ
	[mih**a**nima akt**i**non hi]

Alexander F. Rondos

EMERGENCY

I need help	**Χρειάζομαι βοήθεια**
	[hriazome voithia]
Help!	Βοήθεια
	[voithia]
I am a _____ citizen	Είμαι___πολίτης
	[ime___politis]
Please call the_____Embassy	Παρακαλώ καλέστε την___πρεσβεία
	[parakalo kaleste tin____presvia]
Please call the police	Παρακαλώ καλέστε την αστυνομία
	[parakalo kaleste tin astinomia]
Call an ambulance	Καλέστε ένα ασθενοφόρο
	[kaleste ena asthenoforo]
I need a doctor	Χρειάζομαι έναν γιατρό
	[hriazome enan yatro]
My blood type is _____	Η ομάδα αίματός μου είναι___
	[i omatha ematos mu ine___]
I'm allergic to _____	Είμαι αλεργικός στο___
	[ime aleryikos sto___]
Emergency	Έκτακτη ανάγκη

The Ultimate Greek Phrasebook

	[ektakti anagi]
We need a doctor	Χρειαζόμαστε έναν γιατρό
	[hriazomaste enan yatro]
Evacuate the area	Εκκενώστε την περιοχή
	[ekenoste tin periohi]
Antibiotics	Αντιβιοτικά
	[andiviotika]
Bandage	Επίδεσμος
	[epithesmos]
Blood	Αίμα
	[ema]
Burn	Κάψιμο
	[kapsimo]
Clean	Καθαρό
	[katharo]
Dead	Νεκρός
	[nekros]
Doctor	Γιατρός
	[yatros]
Fever	Πυρετός
	[piretos]
Hospital	Νοσοκομείο
	[nosokomio]
Infection	Μόλυνση

	[m**o**linsi]
Injured	Τραυμαστισμένος
	[travmatism**e**nos]
Medic	Ιατρικό προσωπικό
	[iatrik**o** prosopik**o**]
Medicine	Φάρμακο
	[f**a**rmako]
Nurse	Νοσοκόμα
	[nosok**o**ma]
Poison	Δηλητήριο
	[thilit**i**rio]
Sick	Άρρωστος
	[**a**rostos]
Vitamins	Βιταμίνες
	[vitam**i**nes]
Wound	Τραύμα
	[tr**a**vma]
I am a doctor	Είμαι γιατρός
	[**i**me yatr**os**]
I am not a doctor	Δεν είμαι γιατρός
	[then **i**me yatr**os**]
I am going to help	Θα σας βοηθήσω
	[tha sas voith**i**so]
Can you walk?	Μπορείς να περπατήσεις?

	[boris na perpatisis?]
Can you sit?	Μπορείς να καθίσεις?
	[boris na kathisis?]
Can you stand?	Μπορείς να σταθείς όρθιος?
	[boris na stathis orthios?]
Are you in pain?	Πονάς?
	[ponas?]
I will take you to the hospital	Θα σε πάω στ νοσοκομείο
	[tha se pao sto nosokomio]
Open your mouth	Άνοιξε το στόμα σου
	[anikse to stoma su]
Are you pregnant?	Είσαι έγκυος?
	[ise egios?]

DESCRIPTIONS

Black	**Μαύρο**
	[m<u>a</u>vro]
Blue	Μπλε
	[ble]
Brown	Καφέ
	[kaf<u>e</u>]
Gray	Γκρι
	[gri]
Green	Πράσινο
	[pr<u>a</u>sino]
Orange	Πορτοκαλί
	[portokal<u>i</u>]
Purple	Μωβ
	[mov]
Red	Κόκκινο
	[k<u>o</u>kino]
White	Λευκό
	[lefk<u>o</u>]
Yellow	Κίτρινο
	[k<u>i</u>trino]
Big	Μεγάλο
	[mewh<u>a</u>lo]
Deep	Βαθύ

	[vathi]
Long	Μακρύ
	[makri]
Narrow	Στενό
	[steno]
Short (in height)	Κοντό
	[konto]
Short (in length)	Κοντό
	[konto]
Small	Μικρό
	[mikro]
Large	Μεγάλο
	[mewhalo]
Little	Μικρό
	[mikro]
Tall	Ψηλό
	[psilo]
Thick	Παχύ
	[pahi]
Thin	Λεπτό
	[lepto]
Wide	Πλατύ
	[plati]
Round	Στρογγυλό
	[strogilo]

Straight	Ίσιο/Ευθύ
	[isio/efthi]
Square	Τετράγωνο
	[tetrawhono]
Triangle	Τρίγωνο
	[triwhono]
Bitter	Πικρό
	[pikro]
Fresh	Φρέσκο
	[fresko]
Salty	Αλμυρό
	[almiro]
Sour	Ξινό
	[ksino]
Spicy	Πικάντικο
	[pikandiko]
Sweet	Γλυκό
	[whliko]
Bad	Κακό
	[kako]
Good	Καλό
	[kalo]
Clean	Καθαρό
	[katharo]
Dark	Σκούρο

	[sk**u**ro]
Difficult	Δύσκολο
	[**thi**skolo]
Dirty	Βρώμικό
	[vr**o**miko]
Dry	Ξερό
	[kser**o**]
Easy	Εύκολο
	[**e**fkolo]
Empty	Άδειο
	[**a**thio]
Expensive	Ακριβό
	[akriv**o**]
Fast	Γρήγορο
	[whr**i**whoro]
Full	Γεμάτο
	[yem**a**to]
Hard (firm)	Σφιχτό
	[sfiht**o**]
Heavy	Βαρύ
	[var**i**]
Inexpensive	Φθηνό
	[fthin**o**]
Light (illumination)	Φως
	[fos]

Light (weight)	Ελαφρύ
	[elafr**i**]
Local	Ντόπιο
	[nt**o**pio]
Foreign	Ξένο
	[ks**e**no]
New	Καινούριο
	[ken**u**rio]
Used	Μεταχειρισμένο
	[metahirism**e**no]
Noisy	Θορυβώδες
	[thoriv**o**thes]
Old (about things)	Παλιό
	[pali**o**]
Old (about people)	Γέρος/Γριά
	[y**e**ros (male)/ **whri**a (female)]
Powerful	Δυνατό
	[thinat**o**]
Quiet (person)	Ήσυχος
	[**i**sihos]
Right/correct	Σωστό
	[sost**o**]
Slow	Αργά
	[ar**wha**]

Soft	Μαλακό
	[malako]
Very	Πολύ
	[poli]
Weak	Αδύναμο
	[athinamo]
Wet	Βρεμένο
	[vremeno]
Wrong/incorrect	Λάθος
	[lathos]
Young	Νέος
	[neos]
Few/little	Λίγο
	[liwho]
Many/much	Πολλά/Πολύ
	[pola/ poli]
Part/ Piece	Κομμάτι
	[komati]
Some/a few	Λίγο/ Λίγα
	[liwho/ liwha]
Whole	Ολόκληρο
	[olokliro]

Alexander F. Rondos

Weather

Cold	**Κρύο**
	[kri̱o]
Dry	Ξηρός
	[ksiro̱s]
Earthquake	Σεισμός
	[sismo̱s]
Fog	Ομίχλη
	[omi̱hli]
Hot / Heat	Ζέστη
	[ze̱sti]
Sun	Ήλιος
	[i̱lios]
Humidity	Υγρασία
	[iwhrasi̱a]
Ice	Πάγος
	[pa̱whos]
Lighting	Κεραυνός
	[keravno̱s]
Rain	Βροχή
	[vrohi̱]
Sandstorm	Αμμοθύελα
	[amothi̱ela]
Severe	Σοβαρό

	[sovaro]
Snow	Χιόνι
	[hioni]
Temperature	Θερμοκρασία
	[thermokrasia]
Thunder	Βροντή
	[vronti]
Weather	Καιρός
	[keros]
Rainy	Βροχερός
	[vroheros]

GESTURES

Greek people tend to use their non verbal communication excessively when they talk. Gestures and body movement is such, that a foreigner might be confused when seeing two Greeks talking, thinking that they actually argue! Also, many Greeks are used to talk loud, which is a normal thing for them, so do not be offended or frightened when you encounter them.

Most western gestures have the same meaning in Greece as well. We will guide you through the exceptions and the important ones, in order to avoid finding yourself in an awkward or even dangerous situation during your stay in Greece.

Negative meaning

A very common gesture with negative meaning used in Greece is **moutza**. It is a traditional insult gesture made by extending all five fingers towards the person being insulted. Make sure you don't do that gesture in purpose or accidentally, because the Greeks will find it very offensive. Also, be noted that if the five fingers are towards you (so the other person sees the back of your palm), it means number five.

Fig sign is a gesture which is made with the hand and fingers curled and the thumb thrust between the middle and index fingers, or rarely the middle and ring fingers, forming the fist so that the thumb partly pokes out. In Greece the gesture is considered an obscene gesture, while in other parts of the world is considered a good luck gesture.

Horn sign, is a hand gesture made by extending the index and little finger straight upward. Most of the Greeks will probably connect this with Satan's horns and perceive it negatively.

ILY sign, is a gesture which combines the letters 'I', 'L', and 'Y' by extending the thumb, index finger and little finger, while the middle and ring finger touches the palm. It is an informal expression of love, but again many Greeks will not understand this, and it is possible that they will not even understand its difference with the previous one, the horn sign.

Neutral

Okay, which is made by connecting the thumb and the forefinger in a circle and holding the other fingers straight, is used to signal the word okay. The Greeks are using and will understand this with its proper meaning.

Check, please. This gesture is executed by touching the index finger and thumb together and fictitiously "writing" a checkmark (as if signing his name) in the air. The Greeks are using this gesture a lot, and will understand its proper meaning.

Shrug, a gesture made by lifting both shoulders and indicates lack of knowledge or concern, is also being used by the Greeks a lot, and they will understand its proper meaning

No meaning

Respect, is a gesture which is made by extending the index, middle, and ring fingers of one hand at another person with the middle finger raised slightly higher than the index and ring fingers. It is used in as a sign of respect and approval. Most Greeks will not understand its meaning.

Shocker, is a gesture with sexual connotation. The ring finger and thumb are curled or bent down while the other three fingers are extended. The correspondent Greek gesture is slightly different, and it is made by bending down the middle finger instead of the ring finger, and also not bending the thumb.

V – sign, is made by raising the index and middle fingers and separating them to form a V. With the back of the hand facing outwards this is an offensive gesture in the United Kingdom and some other countries. It is also used in many East Asian nations, as an indication of cuteness when being photographed. In Greece, when the back of the hand is facing outwards, it just means number two. With back of the hand facing inwards, it might mean two, or victory or peace like the rest of the western countries. In no way a Greek will perceive this in a negative way.

Nod, is a gesture made when tilting the head up and down that usually indicates assent in Western Europe, North America, and other places of the world. In Greece it has two different meanings. If the tilt of the head is downwards, then it means yes so it expresses affirmation. When the tilt is done upwards though, usually accompanied by a raise in eyebrows, it means no, declination. So, watch where a Greek is tilting his head, upwards or downwards!

IMPORTANT THINGS TO KNOW

There is no rule for **tipping** in Greece. People do not expect you to tip. Maybe you can tip in coffee houses, restaurants, taverns and maybe room service in hotels, but still it is not compulsory. You can tip as much as you want or nothing at all.

Greece does not have many **public toilets**. If you need to use the toilet you can use any cafeteria's or restaurant's toilet. The law allows you to do that. You do not have to pay for using the toilet anywhere in Greece. Many owners though might resent with that and are not even aware with this law, so consider buying something since the usage of the toilet itself is free. Alternatively, asking if you can use the toilet in a gentle way will do the job, since most professionals (and not only) in Greece would be happy to help a tourist.

Have in mind that the **toilette system** in Greece is not advanced like in other western countries. In most places in Greece you are required not to throw the paper in the toilet, but instead throw it in special small bins next to the toilette, designed for this purpose. These bins are emptied by the cleaning staff, something that is included in their everyday duties.

Payments in Greece are mostly made in cash, so consider having some cash with you at all times.

Most stores and businesses in Greece accept **credit cards**, but don't expect all to do so, since for example, people in small grocery stores or in remote coffee houses or restaurants and in flea markets will probably not accept credit cards. Always check if they do before agreeing on a purchase or using a service.

The official **monetary unit** in Greece is "Euro" and in general no other currency is accepted, so you will have to exchange your currency with euro. You can exchange your currency in banks, currency exchange offices or at the airport.

Using or selling any kind of **drugs** is strictly prohibited in Greece. The country has one of the most strict drug laws in Europe. All citizens and tourists are prohibited to use even light drugs, like marijuana.

Keep your mind for **cars** when you **cross a street**, because car drivers usually ignore pedestrian signs, even crosswalks, except if they stop in red light. Do not expect that car drivers will slow down when you cross the street if they don't have red light. In their mind the pedestrian must wait for the cars to pass first.

Greece is generally a very **safe country**, and no comparison can be made with other European countries or the USA, where safety levels are much lower. Except for some neighborhoods mostly in Athens where it would be preferable not to walk alone at nights, the rest of the country is safe. In smaller cities and villages, crime is almost inexistent.

In case of an **emergency**, dial 100 for police, 166 for hospital care and 199 for fire department. Also, if you have any tourism related problem, like dispute with the hotel owner, you can call the tourist police, who is in charge of these issues and will resolve your issue faster and more efficiently. Tourist police calling number is different in each city or island, so be sure to get it before landing there, or immediately after from the info desk kiosks. If you do not have it, the general tourist police number is 171.

Bread is always included in a meal In Greece. Even if you don't ask for bread in a tavern or a restaurant, the waiter will bring a basket of bread slices in your table, which you will pay extra for (it is not very expensive though).

Although the legal **drinking age limit** in Greece is 18 or 16 under supervision. Most Greeks though do not obey this law. You will see signs at the entrances of some clubs and cafeterias saying that the consumption of alcohol is not permitted to people under 18, but nobody really asks for an identity card when you enter the club or when you order a drink.

Although many Greeks drink frequently, they usually don't forget themselves, so they actually expect you also to be **descent even if you are drunk**. Extreme behaviors and public demonstration of drunkenness is highly disapproved by the Greeks, who might actually call the police if you get too annoying.

In most places of the Greek mainland, the **water** is usually drinkable, but in the islands, you must buy bottled water. Most Greek islands do not have sufficient water reserves, so they have to carry water with tanks. This water is used for other things like bathing or laundering, but not for consumption.

Concerning driving in Greece, an EU or USA driving license is valid, but you must also have an **International Driving Permit** in order to be able to drive.

The **electricity** voltage in Greece is at 220 volts AC and 50Hz. The **plugs** that are used are the round two-pin plugs. Visitors from North America are required to have a transformer and British visitors an adaptor. Some hotels actually provide these adaptors but you can also buy them from most stores with electrical equipment or even at the airport.

FREE E-BOOK "EXPLORE SECRET GREECE" PROMOTION

Did you really like the "Ultimate Greek Phrasebook"? Would you be interested in learning about hidden places in Greece, like isolated beaches, uninhabited islands, medieval cities and castles, unknown picturesque villages, a hidden butterfly valley, an exotic palm tree beach and much more?

If so, my e-book "Explore Secret Greece – 50+1 Hidden gems only locals know" can be yours for free as a part of my promotion!

If you truly liked the "Ultimate Greek Phrasebook", and you would like to share this opinion with others by posting a review to the store you bought this book from, we will be happy to compensate you for your time and your confidence to us by sending you the "Explore Secret Greece" for free. For example, if you bought the Ultimate Greek Phrasebook from Amazon.com, the procedure would be the following:

1. Go to the store that you bought the book from (for now only Amazon verified purchase comments are eligible for free Explore Secret Greece book), e.g. Amazon.com, and post a 5 star positive review on the Ultimate Greek Phrasebook. Sincerely write the reasons you liked the book, and how it helped you in planning or in your actual trip to Greece, or in learning Greek. The comment must come from a verified purchase. For example, if you have purchased the book from Amazon, and you write the review using the same account, the purchase will automatically be verified. You are eligible for the free e-book whether you have a kindle or a paperback version of "The Ultimate Greek Phrasebook".

2. Email me at **xpressepublishing@gmail.com** In the email subject write "I am interested about the free Explore Secret Greece e-book" and in the email body write: "My name is Alex Rondos (replace with your name) and I have bought the Ultimate Greek Phrasebook from Amazon.com. My Amazon.com nickname is "Alex.Rondos" (replace with the name that is visible when you comment and post reviews on the store that you bought the book from) and I have just commented positively on your Book at www.amazon.com. Please send me my free "Explore Secret Greece" e-book. There are other ways you can contact me through my Webpage and through Facebook. Please see at the end of this book.
3. After verifying your review, we will email you the "Explore Secret Greece" e-book in .pdf format and written permission to print the book one time for your own use. We try to reply all requests within 48 hours. Make sure to check your spam folder as well in case your email provider falsely lists our email address as spam.

Please note that in no case we want you to post a positive review if you did not like our book. In that case, we urge you to contact us and explain why you did not like the book. We carefully listen to our readers in order to improve future editions of our books.

Thank you *for reading this book. Please make sure you keep it with you at all times during your staying in Greece. Have a nice time, and don't forget to contact us for any question or note at* ***xpressepublishing@gmail.com****!!*

Also, be sure to follow us at

http://theultimategreekphrasebook.wordpress.com/

and

https://www.facebook.com/greekphrasebook

for the latest newsfeed.

Made in the USA
Las Vegas, NV
20 March 2024